COOKING
THE
INDIAN
WAY

This book is available in two editions:
Library binding by Lerner Publications Company,
    a division of Lerner Publishing Group
Soft cover by First Avenue Editions,
    an imprint of Lerner Publishing Group
241 First Avenue North
Minneapolis, MN 55401 U.S.A.

Website address: www.lernerbooks.com

Library of Congress Cataloging-in-Publication Data

Madavan, Vijay.
    Cooking the Indian way / by Vijay Madavan—Rev. & expanded.
        p.   cm. — (Easy menu ethnic cookbooks)
    Includes index.
    Summary: An introduction to the cuisine and culture of India, including information about the country's social life and customs.
    ISBN: 0–8225–4110–6 (lib. bdg. : alk. paper)
    ISBN: 0–8225–0534–7 (pbk. : alk. paper)
    1. Cookery, India—Juvenile literature. 2. India—Social life and customs—Juvenile literature. [1. Cookery, India. 2. India—Social life and customs.] I. Title. II. Series.
TX724.5.I4 M26 2002
641.5954—dc21   2001004240

Manufactured in the United States of America
1 2 3 4 5 6 – AM – 07 06 05 04 03 02

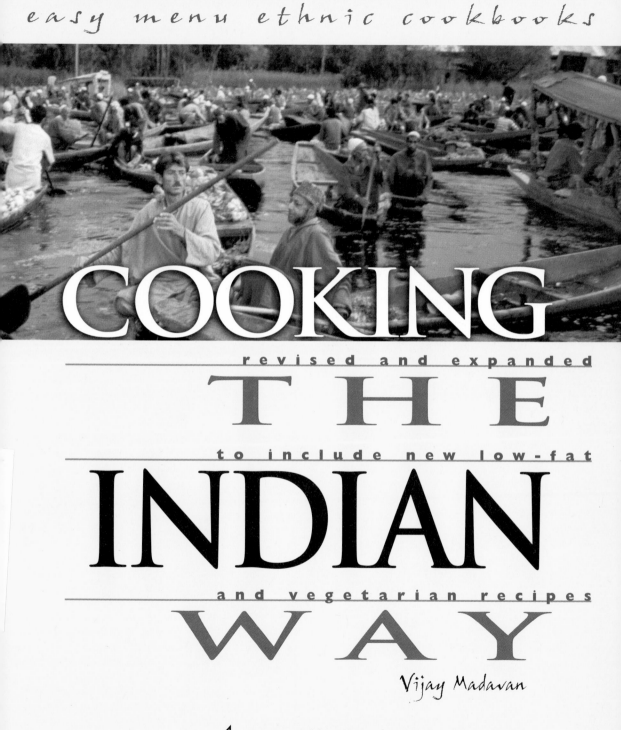

easy menu ethnic cookbooks

COOKING

revised and expanded

THE

to include new low-fat

INDIAN

and vegetarian recipes

WAY

Vijay Madavan

Ŀ Lerner Publications Company • Minneapolis

Contents

Introduction

India, like many countries, has dramatic contrasts in geography, climate, and population. Within the territory of this vast country are dense forests, arid deserts, fertile plains, humid tropical coasts fringed with tall coconut palms, and the snow-covered peaks of some of the world's highest mountains. The weather during a typical Indian year includes scorching heat, with temperatures up to 120°F (49°C), and drenching monsoon rains. These conditions allow India's agricultural industry to produce the variety of foods commonly used in the country's cuisine. How these ingredients are prepared often depends on the ethnic and religious practices of the people cooking and eating the food. Preparing and eating Indian foods is one way to become acquainted with this fabulous country without ever leaving home. The recipes in this book will get you started on a voyage of discovery that you will never forget.

Combining almost any variety of lentil—or several—with garlic and onions produces a satisfying vegetarian dish. (Recipe on page 50.)

AFGHANISTAN

PAKISTAN

JAMMU
AND
KASHMIR

Indus River

Delhi

HIMALAYAS

CHINA

NEPAL

Ganges River

BHUTAN

Brahmaputra River

BANGLADESH

Kolkata
(Calcutta)

MYANMAR
(BURMA)

INDIA

Mumbai
(Bombay)

WESTERN GHATS

Godavari River

Arabian Sea

Krishna River

EASTERN GHATS

Bangalore

Bay of Bengal

SRI
LANKA

Disputed
boundary

The People of India

The people of India, like the land they live in, are remarkably varied.
Most Indians who live in the southern part of the country are
descendants of the land's earliest inhabitants, who created a rich
civilization in the Indus River valley around 2500 B.C. The people of
northern India are descended from later invaders who pushed the
original inhabitants south as they established their empires.

Modern Indians differ in their styles of living as well. Many Indians make their homes in tiny rural villages centered around a single well. Others live in cities like Mumbai (Bombay) and Kolkata (Calcutta) that are among the largest in the world. Most Indians are farmers who raise crops for their own use, but some run large businesses, teach at universities, or work in India's busy motion picture industry.

India's one billion inhabitants speak 14 major languages and more than 1,000 minor tongues. Hindi is the nation's official language, but many Indians know it only as a second language. With their families and friends, they may speak Bengali, Punjabi, Tamil, Telugu, or another of India's many ancient tongues with its own traditions and literature.

Most Indians—about 82 percent—are followers of Hinduism, an ancient, polytheistic religion (a religion whose adherents worship more than one god). Muslims, followers of Islam (the religion established in the seventh century A.D. by the prophet Muhammad, make up 12 percent of the population. Practitioners of several other religions, such as Sikhism and Jainism, make up the rest of the population. Although some modern Indians no longer observe all their religion's rules governing diet, styles of dress, marriage and family life, and occupations, many still follow the religious traditions of their ancestors.

Indian Food's Varied Traditions

The food of India clearly—and deliciously—reflects the great variety of Indian life. What people eat depends on the crops raised in the area, the ethnic and religious traditions of the inhabitants, and the simplicity or sophistication of their lifestyles. These variations create a fascinating and unique cuisine.

Geography and climate have an important influence on Indian foods. The wide plains and dry climate of northern India produce large quantities of wheat. *Chapatis* and *puris*, wheat breads, are a staple of the diet in this region. Rice grows well in southern India's humid climate. Along its miles of coastline, seafood and tropical fruits such as bananas and coconuts are typical fare too.

Differences in diet also stem from the historical and religious backgrounds of northern and southern India. Muslim armies led a series of military and cultural conquests in northern India, starting in the seventh century A.D. They brought with them their Muslim faith and distinctive cuisine. Northern Indians still cook many delicious dishes containing lamb, yogurt, and other ingredients typical of the cuisines the invaders brought with them.

Because invaders rarely made it as far as southern India, the people of the south preserved more of their early, primarily Hindu, culture. The emphasis in this region on fresh-cooked vegetables and strong spices represents classic Indian cooking.

Spices: India's Treasures

The spices of India have been famous for centuries. When Europeans ventured into this part of the world in the early 1500s, they came seeking the treasures of the region: pepper, cinnamon, saffron, ginger, and cloves. Every Indian household uses these spices daily.

People of Western countries often think Indian spices are hot. Actually, spices such as cumin, coriander, and turmeric have a rich, mellow taste with only a mild bite. Indian food gets its heat from chilies, the same fiery peppers used in Mexican cooking. If you don't share this fondness for hot food, use fewer chilies than the recipe calls for or omit them. This will not affect the wonderful flavor of the unique Indian spices in the dish.

Most cooking methods used in India are well known to Western cooks, but some methods of preparation may be unfamiliar. For instance, some of the recipes in this book call for whole spices, such as cumin seeds or cardamom pods, to be cooked in hot oil

Many recipes originating in southern India feature rice, which is often cultivated in terraced paddies like this.

first. This technique brings out a different flavor than does using ground spices or whole, uncooked spices.

When dishes call for ground spices, Indian cooks grind them fresh. You can use already ground spices from the supermarket, but you may want to try grinding whole spices yourself to experience the marvelous flavor they give to Indian dishes.

The easiest method of grinding whole spices is to use a small electric grinder of the kind used to grind coffee beans or nuts. (An electric blender can also be used, although the mixture will not be as fine.) You should start with about the same amount of whole spice as the amount of ground spice called for in the recipe. Grind the amount needed for about 30 seconds, until it is a fine powder.

Indian cooks often combine their freshly ground spices into a special blend called *garam masala.* This spice mixture is usually added to dishes near the end of the cooking or used as a garnish. Each cook has his or her own recipe for garam masala, but most contain some combination of cumin, cardamom, cinnamon, and cloves. Start with the garam masala recipe on page 35 and develop your own.

Women paint the streets with rice powder in preparation for Pongal. This annual rice harvest festival is the biggest event of the year in southern India.

Holidays and Festivals

Numerous holidays and festivals spice the Indian calendar, highlighting the country's culturally diverse populace. Almost every day, somewhere in India, a celebration takes place. These occasions may honor historical events, religious symbols, deities, gurus, harvests, or seasons. Most festivals in India began as Hindu holidays, but in modern times these events combine religious, seasonal, and regional elements. Although the name and purpose for each event vary throughout India, feasts and high spirits abound.

All of India glows during Diwali—the festival of lights—which usually falls in October. The rituals associated with Diwali symbolize the defeat of spiritual darkness. Families whitewash their homes and adorn them with colorful designs, oil lamps, and candles. They rise before dawn, cleanse themselves in oil baths, and dress in new clothes. Since the festival is a day for visitors, presentability is key. Indians tour streets brightened by garlands of lights and exchange sweets (as symbols of prosperity) with friends and neighbors.

Three-fourths of the country's population depend on agriculture for their livelihood. Farmers devote much of India's land to rice production—a staple in the south and east. Pongal (thanksgiving for the winter rice harvest) is the biggest festival of the year in southern India. Lasting three to four days in mid-January, the celebration centers around the preparation and distribution of a special dish, also called *pongal*. On the first day, after the rice harvest, women cook the grain outdoors in special mud pots. Households purchase these pots—*pongapani*—each year for the festival at a village market. The pongapani boast colorful designs. The neck of each pot wears a tie of fresh, green turmeric and ginger plants. The leaves of the plants represent prosperity; turmeric, good things to come; and ginger, the spice of life. Inside the pot, rice, milk, *dal* (lentils or other legumes), nuts, and other special ingredients are brought to a boil until the liquid overflows, an announcement of bounty.

In thanksgiving to those who contributed to the success of the rice crop, Indians offer pongal. They also offer sugarcane to insure sweetness and happiness in the coming season. First they offer the rain and sun gods a portion. Then farmers show appreciation to their cattle by bathing them, painting their horns, and adorning them with beads, bells, and flower necklaces. The beautified cattle feast on the pongal dish, and the birds that keep the insects under control are offered a bite as well. Families then gather with friends and neighbors to share in a pongal meal. By the end of Pongal, everyone has had a chance to taste the delicious fruits of their labor.

Originally celebrated only in farming communities, harvest festivals have gained popularity throughout India. Two occasions similar to Pongal—Sankranti and Lohri—appear in the central and northern parts of the country. Rice and til (sesame seeds) star in Sankranti's tasty dishes of khichadi (rice and dal) and bajari (bread and til). People exchange tilgul—balls of fried, sweetened sesame seeds—with the words "Speak sweetly."

Lohri falls in the winter, and people celebrate around a large bonfire. Not all food at Indian festivals is meant to be eaten. Children spend Lohri collecting sweets, puffed rice, and popcorn from neighbors and toss these goodies into the fire for good luck.

Most people have never seen anything quite like Holi, which begins with a bonfire. In general, Holi celebrates spring's arrival with good-humored abandon. Indians of all castes (social classes) gather in the streets to honor the colors of spring. Revelers douse each other in gulal—vibrantly colored powders and liquids. Luckily everybody wears grubby outfits, because soon all of India is stained in festive hues. This occasion cements a spirit of camaraderie and love throughout the country.

As a rite of spring, Holi also honors Krishna—a Hindu deity with a jovial, flirty reputation. Krishna adored milk products. In his memory, pots of buttermilk are suspended between buildings. Young men gather on the street below to form human pyramids. The first person to reach a buttermilk pot is crowned the king of Holi. The rest of the revelers seek safer refreshment in thandai, a nutty milk beverage that's perfect after an active festival day.

Muslims comprise the second largest religious group in India, and their holidays and festivals correspond to those of Islamic communities around the world. Eid al-Fitr follows a 30-day fast called Ramadan. During this month, Muslims abstain from food and drink from sunrise to sunset. They devote the days to intensive prayer and worship. On the first day of the following month, Muslims eat dates at sunrise, thus breaking the fast. Later in the day, families and friends gather for an elaborate feast. The menu always

Holi revelers in New Delhi honor the jovial Hindu deity Krishna by cheerfully staining each other with gulal—vibrantly colored powders and liquids.

includes sweetened vermicelli called *sevian*. *Kebabs*, *biryani*, and *malpua* usually make an appearance as well. After a month-long fast, the delicacies taste even better.

Holidays and festivals foster a sense of community and pride among India's diverse peoples. The enjoyment that comes from preparing special dishes and sharing delicious food with family, friends, and neighbors is a central ingredient of India's colorful festivals and holidays.

Before You Begin

Indian cooking makes use of some ingredients that you may not know. Sometimes special cookware is also used, although the recipes in this book can easily be prepared with ordinary utensils and pans.

The most important thing you need to know before you start is how to be a careful cook. On the following page, you'll find a few rules that will make your cooking experience safe, fun, and easy. Next, take a look at the "dictionary" of utensils, terms, and special ingredients. You may also want to read the section on preparing healthy, low-fat meals.

When you've picked out a recipe to try, read through it from beginning to end. You will then be ready to shop for ingredients and to organize the cookware you will need. Once you have assembled everything, you'll be ready to begin cooking.

Kebabs made from ground lamb or beef are delicious prepared over an outdoor charcoal grill, and they are easy to serve. (Recipe on page 40.)

The Careful Cook

Whenever you cook, there are certain safety rules you must always keep in mind. Even experienced cooks follow these rules when they are in the kitchen.

- Always wash your hands before handling food. Thoroughly wash all raw vegetables and fruits to remove dirt, chemicals, and insecticides. Wash uncooked poultry, meats, and fish under cold water.
- Use a cutting board when cutting up vegetables and fruits. Don't cut them up in your hand! And be sure to cut in a direction *away* from you and your fingers.
- Long hair or loose clothing can easily catch fire if brought near the burners of a stove. If you have long hair, tie it back before you start cooking.
- Turn all pot handles toward the back of the stove so that you will not catch your sleeves or jewelry on them. This is especially important when younger brothers and sisters are around. They could easily knock off a pot and get burned.
- Always use a pot holder to steady hot pots or to take pans out of the oven. Don't use a wet cloth on a hot pan because the steam it produces could burn you.
- Lift the lid of a steaming pot with the opening away from you so that you will not get burned.
- If you get burned, hold the burn under cold running water. Do not put grease or butter on it. Cold water helps to take the heat out, but grease or butter will only keep it in.
- If grease or cooking oil catches fire, throw baking soda or salt at the bottom of the flame to put it out. (Water will *not* put out a grease fire.) Call for help, and try to turn all the stove burners to "off."

- Handle fresh chilies with care because they contain oils that can burn your eyes or mouth. After working with chilies, be sure not to touch your face until you have washed your hands thoroughly with soap and water. To be extra cautious, wear rubber gloves while fixing chilies. The way you cut the peppers will affect their hotness. If you take out the seeds, the flavor will be sharp but not fiery. If you leave the seeds in, beware!

Cooking Utensils

colander/sieve—A bowl-shaped dish with holes in it used for washing or draining food

electric grinder—A small, electric appliance used for grinding hard, dry foods such as spices, coffee beans, and grains

skewer—A thin metal or wooden rod used to hold small pieces of food for broiling or grilling

slotted spoon—A spoon with small openings in the bowl used to scoop solid food out of a liquid

spatula—A flat, thin utensil, usually metal, used to lift, toss, turn, or scoop food

Cooking Terms

beat—To stir rapidly in a circular motion

boil—To heat a liquid until bubbles form and rise rapidly to the surface

fillet—A boneless piece of fish or meat

garnish—To decorate with small pieces of food

knead—To work dough by pressing it with the palms, pushing it outward, and then pressing it over on itself

paste—A smooth, creamy mixture made by grinding ingredients together

roast—To cook in an open pan in an oven so heat penetrates the food from all sides

rub—To mix solid fat into flour until it has a coarse, mealy texture

simmer—To cook over low heat in liquid kept just below its boiling point

Special Ingredients

basmati rice—a long-grained rice with a delicate, nutty flavor

cayenne pepper—Dried red chilies that have been ground to make a fine powder

chickpeas—Also known as garbanzo beans, chickpeas are found in the dry beans or canned foods section of a supermarket.

chilies—Spicy relatives of the familiar green, or bell, pepper, chilies are what make Indian food hot. The fresh green chili, a slim, bright-green pepper, can often be obtained in the produce department of a large supermarket or canned in the Mexican food section of many groceries.

coconut milk—Available canned at stores that specialize in Indian or Asian food, this product is not the milk from the inside of a coconut, but a juice made from steeping coconut meat in water. If it isn't available, coconut milk can be made by soaking flaked coconut in boiling water for 5 minutes (or blending it in boiling water for 1 minute), then straining out the coconut flakes. Lite coconut milk, with less fat and fewer calories, is available in most groceries.

fresh coriander—This fresh green herb is used to add flavor and color to many Indian dishes. Under the name cilantro, it is also popular in Mexican cooking. Most large supermarkets carry fresh coriander in their produce departments, right next to the parsley.

garlic—An herb whose strong distinctive flavor is used in many dishes. Fresh garlic can be found in the produce department of a supermarket. Each bulb, or head, can be broken up into several small sections called cloves. Before you chop up a clove of garlic, you will have to remove the brittle, papery cover that surrounds it.

ghee—A type of butter, also called clarified butter, that no longer contains milk solids. Indian cooks prefer ghee to traditional butter because it doesn't become rancid or smoke when heated to high temperatures. Butter or oil will work for the recipes in this book.

ginger root—A knobby, light brown root used to flavor food. To use fresh ginger root, slice off the amount called for, peel off the skin with the side of a spoon, and grate the flesh. Freeze the rest of the root for future use. Fresh ginger has a very zippy taste, so use it sparingly. (Do not substitute dried ground ginger in a recipe calling for fresh ginger, as the taste is very different.)

jaggery—A coarse brown sugar commonly used in Indian cooking that tastes similar to a sweeter molasses

SPICES

black mustard seeds—These seeds can be found in Indian markets or health food stores. Yellow seeds may be substituted, using a smaller quantity of this stronger variety.

cardamom pods—A whole spice used in Indian cooking. To use, remove the seeds from the pods and discard the shell.

curry leaves—An herb that resembles small bay leaves and smells like lime. Usually found only in Indian markets, they may be omitted.

fenugreek—Difficult to find outside of Indian or Middle Eastern markets, this slightly bitter herb adds a unique flavor, but can be omitted without harm to the recipe.

garam masala—An Indian spice mixture that can be purchased at Indian stores and some supermarkets in dry or paste form. Most Indian cooks make their own garam masala, and personal preference dictates the ratio of seasonings.

turmeric—A ground spice that turns food a brilliant yellow hue and tastes bitter in excess

Healthy and Low-Fat Cooking Tips

Many modern cooks are concerned about preparing healthy, low-fat meals. Fortunately, there are simple ways to reduce the fat content of most dishes. Here are a few general tips for adapting the recipes in this book. Throughout the book, you'll also find specific suggestions for individual recipes—and don't worry, they'll still taste delicious!

Many recipes call for butter or oil to sauté vegetables or other ingredients. Using oil lowers saturated fat right away, but you can also reduce the amount of oil you use. You can also substitute a low-fat or nonfat cooking spray for oil. Sprinkling a little salt on the vegetables brings out their natural juices, so less oil is needed. It's also a good idea to use a small, nonstick frying pan if you decide to use less oil than the recipe calls for.

Dairy products like yogurt and milk are a common source of unwanted fat. Both items are available in reduced or nonfat varieties (2% milk has more fat than skim). Another easy way to reduce the amount of fat from dairy products is simply to use smaller amounts! Also, health food stores and natural foods sections of large groceries carry rice milk and soy milks, cheeses, and yogurts. People around the world enjoy these delicious foods as low-fat alternatives to dairy products. You may want to experiment with substituting these items.

Some cooks like to replace ground beef with ground turkey to lower fat. However, since this does change the flavor, you may need to experiment a little bit to decide if you like this substitution. Buying extra-lean ground beef is also an easy way to reduce fat.

There are many ways to prepare meals that are good for you and still taste great. As you become a more experienced cook, try experimenting with recipes and substitutions to find the methods that work best for you.

METRIC CONVERSIONS

Cooks in the United States measure both liquid and solid ingredients using standard containers based on the 8-ounce cup and the tablespoon. These measurements are based on volume, while the metric system of measurement is based on both weight (for solids) and volume (for liquids). To convert from U.S. fluid tablespoons, ounces, quarts, and so forth to metric liters is a straightforward conversion, using the chart below. However, since solids have different weights—one cup of rice does not weigh the same as one cup of grated cheese, for example—many cooks who use the metric system have kitchen scales to weigh different ingredients. The chart below will give you a good starting point for basic conversions to the metric system.

MASS (weight)

1 ounce (oz.)	=	28.0 grams (g)
8 ounces	=	227.0 grams
1 pound (lb.) or 16 ounces	=	0.45 kilograms (kg)
2.2 pounds	=	1.0 kilogram

LIQUID VOLUME

1 teaspoon (tsp.)	=	5.0 milliliters (ml)
1 tablespoon (tbsp.)	=	15.0 milliliters
1 fluid ounce (oz.)	=	30.0 milliliters
1 cup (c.)	=	240 milliliters
1 pint (pt.)	=	480 milliliters
1 quart (qt.)	=	0.95 liters (l)
1 gallon (gal.)	=	3.80 liters

LENGTH

¼ inch (in.)	=	0.6 centimeters (cm)
½ inch	=	1.25 centimeters
1 inch	=	2.5 centimeters

TEMPERATURE

212°F	=	100°C (boiling point of water)
225°F	=	110°C
250°F	=	120°C
275°F	=	135°C
300°F	=	150°C
325°F	=	160°C
350°F	=	180°C
375°F	=	190°C
400°F	=	200°C

(To convert temperature in Fahrenheit to Celsius, subtract 32 and multiply by .56)

PAN SIZES

8-inch cake pan	= 20 x 4-centimeter cake pan
9-inch cake pan	= 23 x 3.5-centimeter cake pan
11 x 7-inch baking pan	= 28 x 18-centimeter baking pan
13 x 9-inch baking pan	= 32.5 x 23-centimeter baking pan
9 x 5-inch loaf pan	= 23 x 13-centimeter loaf pan
2-quart casserole	= 2-liter casserole

An Indian Table

To eat Indian style, seat your guests on the floor. Give each person a tray of foods in small dishes. Indians eat with their fingers, using bread to scoop up other foods or shaping bite-sized balls of rice in the sauce of another dish. If you would like to give this a try too, be sure to have wet cloths or finger bowls handy.

Given the great variety of food and styles of eating in India, there is no one pattern for daily meals in India. What and when people eat depends on where they live, on the religious laws they observe, and on their financial situation. In general, most Indians have one main meal a day, usually between 12 and 2 P.M., and several smaller meals. Breakfast may consist of lentils and bread or yogurt, always accompanied by tea. Afternoon tea is a custom in many parts of India, and most Indians also enjoy snacking on salty, seasoned treats sold by street vendors. The day ends with a light evening meal of several simple dishes—for example, rice and lentils—usually eaten after 8 P.M.

Indian women congregate to cook flat unleavened whole wheat bread at a spring festival. (Recipe on pages 54–55.)

An Indian Menu

For most Indians, the big meal of the day consists of small portions of many dishes instead of one main dish. According to Indian custom, the main recipes in this book are divided into vegetarian and non-vegetarian categories. You will also find recipes for accompanying dishes such as chutneys, breads, *raitas*, and pulses (lentils and peas) that could be eaten with both kinds of meals. Desserts are not usually included in daily meals, but on special occasions Indians enjoy eating candylike sweets made from milk. For your first taste of Indian food, you might choose just one dish, for example, spicy fried fish, and serve it with a vegetable and a green salad, or try one of the following menus.

LUNCH

Pastries (stuffed with potatoes and peas)

Fresh coriander chutney

Yogurt chicken

Carrots with grated coconut

Banana yogurt

Unleavend whole wheat bread

SHOPPING LIST:

Produce

4 green chilies
2 bunches fresh coriander (cilantro)
1 small fresh ginger root
1 bulb garlic
6 carrots
2 bananas
1 lemon
1 onion
3 potatoes

Dairy/Egg/Meat

3½–4 lbs. chicken pieces
plain yogurt
1 stick butter or margarine

Canned/Bottled/Boxed

vegetable oil
1 10-oz. package frozen peas
2 oz. cashews, for garnish
2 oz. ground peanuts, for garnish

Miscellaneous

6 oz. flaked or grated coconut
salt
ground cumin
ground coriander
ground turmeric
cinnamon or garam masala
black or yellow mustard seeds
black pepper
whole-wheat flour
all-purpose flour

VEGETARIAN MEAL

Pumpkin curry

Plain rice

Curried chickpeas

Cucumber and mint yogurt

Lassi

SHOPPING LIST:

Produce

1 small pumpkin or winter
   squash
1 onion
1 bulb garlic
1 small fresh ginger root
1 bunch fresh coriander
   (cilantro)
1 cucumber
1 bunch fresh mint
1 green chili (optional)

Dairy/Egg/Meat

1 stick butter or margarine
plain yogurt

Canned/Bottled/Boxed

4 oz. coconut milk
vegetable oil
12 oz. dried chickpeas or 2
   14-oz. cans presoaked
   chickpeas

Miscellaneous

8 oz. lentils, brown or split
   red
basmati rice
cayenne pepper
ground cumin
ground turmeric
salt
ground fenugreek
black mustard seeds
1 curry leaf (optional)
ground coriander
cumin seeds
garam masala (optional)
black pepper

Snacks and Beverages

Snacks are popular in India. Hungry moviegoers may munch on *samosas*, fried stuffed pastries—a favorite movie theater concession—as they watch a recent release from India's billion-dollar movie industry.

On crowded city streets, vendors peddle a selection of tasty on-the-go food. They sell *kheema*, seasoned meat, as well as salty, crunchy mixtures of nuts and pulses. They make these treats on site with portable cookware and fresh ingredients from roadside markets. Vendors also offer glasses of brightly colored *sharbats*, sweet drinks made with sugar and flavorings such as mint and sandalwood.

Indians drink many kinds of beverages. In southern India, coffee is the preferred beverage, and many households grind coffee beans fresh every day. Tea is grown in northern India, where it is often served with cinnamon and cloves. Many Indian dishes can burn the tongue, so Indians often respond with salty, creamy beverages such as cold buttermilk or a yogurt drink called *lassi* (see recipe on page 36).

A marvelously versatile Indian appetizer is a samosa stuffed with vegetables or meat. (Recipe on pages 30–31.)

Stuffed Pastries / Samosas

Samosas are a favorite snack food in India. These little pastries are perfect for eating with your fingers and make a good appetizer to start an Indian meal. Try dipping them in coriander chutney (see recipe on page 60). Samosas can be stuffed with many kinds of meat or vegetable fillings.*

Dough:

½ c. all-purpose flour

½ c. whole-wheat flour

¼ tsp. salt

1 tbsp. butter or margarine

up to ½ c. water

about 1 c. vegetable oil (for frying)

about 2 c. filling (see recipes on pages 32–33)

1. Put all-purpose flour, whole wheat flour, and salt in a mixing bowl. Cut butter into small pieces and add to flour. Rub butter into flour with your fingertips until mixture looks like large bread crumbs. Mix in enough water, a little at a time, to form a firm dough.

2. Knead dough in bowl for about 2 or 3 minutes, or until smooth. Cover bowl and refrigerate while making filling.

3. When filling is ready, remove dough from refrigerator and place on a floured surface. Knead dough for about 5 minutes.

4. Divide dough into pieces about the size of walnuts and roll each piece into a smooth ball with your hands.

5. Roll balls into thin rounds with a floured rolling pin. Cut each round in half.

6. Put about 1 tbsp. filling onto a piece of dough. Fold dough over filling. Seal edges of dough with your fingers and then with the tines of a fork. Continue making samosas.

7. In a wok or a deep saucepan, heat oil over medium-high heat. (Oil should be deep enough to cover samosas while cooking.) Carefully place one samosa in oil. If samosa fries to a golden brown in about 3 minutes, the oil is at the right temperature. If it takes longer than this, increase temperature of oil. When oil is at the right temperature, continue frying samosas, a few at a time, for 3 minutes each. Remove samosas with a slotted spoon and drain on paper towels. Eat hot or at room temperature.

Preparation time: 60 minutes
Cooking time: 20 to 25 minutes
Yields 10 to 15 samosas

*Kheema (recipe on page 33) makes a spicy meat filling. For vegetarian samosas, fill the pastries with potatoes and peas (recipe on page 32). To avoid unwanted fat, bake rather than deep-fry the samosas. Place the stuffed triangles on a cookie sheet, brush each with a little butter or oil, and bake at 350°F until they turn golden brown (about 10 to 15 minutes).

Potatoes and Peas / Aloo Mattar

This savory mixture of potatoes and peas can be eaten as part of a vegetarian meal or served with chapatis (see recipe on pages 54–55) for lunch or a snack. It also makes an excellent filling for samosas (see recipe on pages 30–31).

2 tbsp. vegetable or peanut oil

1 green chili, chopped

1 tsp. chopped fresh ginger

1 clove garlic, chopped

1 small onion, chopped

½ tsp. salt

3 large potatoes, peeled and chopped

2 c. water

1 10-oz. package frozen peas, thawed, or 1 17-oz. can green peas, drained

¼ c. cashews for garnish

1. In a large skillet, heat oil over medium-high heat. Add chili, ginger, garlic, onion, and salt and fry about 3 minutes, stirring frequently, or until mixture is brown and fragrant.

2. Add potatoes and water and stir to combine. Cover skillet, lower heat, and simmer about 20 minutes, or until potatoes are tender.

3. When potatoes are cooked, add peas and simmer 3 minutes, or until peas are heated through.

4. Serve potatoes and peas hot, or at room temperature with cashews sprinkled on top.

Preparation time: 20 minutes
Cooking time: 25 to 30 minutes
Serves 4 to 6

Spiced Ground Meat / *Kheema*

Kheema is a very popular dish all over northern India. In the cities, it is sold at stands in the streets and is often eaten as a quick snack or lunch. In its basic ingredients, kheema is similar to the hamburger casseroles often served in Western homes, but the Indian spices give it a uniquely rich flavor.

1 lb. ground lamb or beef

1 tbsp. garam masala (recipe on
    page 35) or 1 tsp. each pepper,
    ground cloves, and ground cumin

½ tsp. salt

3 tbsp. vegetable oil

½ medium onion, thinly sliced

3 cloves garlic, chopped

1 tbsp. chopped fresh ginger

3 cardamom pods

1 stick cinnamon

2 medium potatoes, peeled and
    chopped

1 c. water

1 green chili, chopped

2 medium tomatoes, chopped

1 10-oz. package frozen peas,
    thawed, or 1 17-oz. can green
    peas, drained

fresh coriander for garnish

1. In a bowl, mix together meat, garam masala, and salt.

2. Heat oil in a large skillet over medium-high heat. Add onion, garlic, ginger, cardamom, and cinnamon and fry about 5 minutes, or until onions turn brown. Add meat mixture and stir until meat is completely brown.

3. Add potatoes and water, lower heat, and simmer about 20 minutes, or until potatoes are tender and liquid has cooked off.

4. Add chili, tomatoes, and peas and stir to combine. Cook for about 5 minutes to heat through.

5. Remove skillet from heat. Remove cardamom pods and cinnamon stick from skillet. Garnish kheema with coriander leaves and serve steaming hot.

Preparation time: 15 to 20 minutes
Cooking time: 45 minutes
Serves 6 to 8

Garam Masala

3 sticks cinnamon

½ c. cardamom pods

¼ c. whole cloves

¼ c. cumin seeds

2 tbsp. coriander seeds

¼ c. black peppercorns

1 tbsp. ground ginger

1. Preheat oven to 200°F. Roast all ingredients except ginger in an ungreased 9 × 13-inch baking pan on bottom oven rack for 30 minutes. Stir several times.

2. Remove from oven and let cool.

3. Use your fingers to break open cardamom pods. Remove seeds and discard pods.

4. With a rolling pin, crush the cinnamon sticks between two towels or in a plastic bag.

5. Combine all spices except ginger in a bowl and mix well.

6. Grind the mixture in an electric grinder or blender* until it's a fine powder (about 30 seconds).

7. Add ground ginger and mix well.

8. Stored in a sealed jar at room temperature, garam masala will stay fresh for up to six months.

*If you use an electric blender, your garam masala will be fairly coarse. You may also use a traditional tool called a mortar and pestle, a bowl and thick grinding stick (pictured on page 34).

Cooking time: 30 minutes
Preparation time: 20 minutes
Makes 1 cup

Spiced Tea / Masala Chai

3 c. water

2 sticks cinnamon

15 cardamom pods

15 whole cloves

1 tbsp. chopped fresh ginger

3 tbsp. black tea leaves

1 c. milk

3 tbsp. sugar

1. In a medium saucepan, bring water, cinnamon, cardamom, cloves, and ginger to a boil over medium-high heat. Turn off heat, add tea, and cover pan. Let stand for 3 minutes.

2. Strain liquid into another saucepan. Add milk and sugar. Bring to a boil over medium-high heat.

3. As soon as tea begins to boil, pour into cups. Serve immediately.

Preparation time: 10 minutes
Serves 4 to 6

Lassi

1 c. plain yogurt

1½ c. ice-cold water

1 tsp. salt

1 tsp. ground cumin

1 green chili, finely chopped (optional)

1. Combine all ingredients in a blender and blend about 15 seconds, or until frothy. (If you don't have a blender, place all ingredients in a tightly covered jar and shake to mix.)

2. Pour into glasses and serve immediately.

Preparation time: 10 minutes
Serves 2 to 3

*To whip up a fruit lassi, replace the salt, cumin, and chili with 2 ripe bananas or half a mango and 2 tbsp. sugar.

Spiced tea is an aromatic hot beverage that complements many Indian dishes.

Meat and Fish

Among Indians who choose to eat meat, religious affiliation often dictates which animals they may consume. Muslims are forbidden by their religion to eat any pork or pork products, but they are allowed to have beef and other kinds of meat. Lamb kebabs and yogurt chicken reveal a Muslim influence at the Indian table.

Hindus, in contrast, never eat beef because the cow is considered a sacred animal in the Hindu faith. Spicy fried fish is typical traditional cuisine among meat-eating Hindus. Frequently, the meat prepared in Indian homes consists of a few small pieces stewed in thick sauces much like those common in vegetarian curry dishes. Many devout Hindus eat no meat at all and are strict vegetarians, avoiding even seafood and eggs.

A chicken-based entrée sidesteps the dietary prohibitions of many spiritual practices in India, and cooking chicken with yogurt makes a succulent main course. (Yogurt chicken recipe on page 41.)

Ground Lamb Kebabs/ *Kabab Masala*

Kebabs, meat cooked on skewers, are eaten throughout northern India. This recipe uses ground lamb or beef that is molded around the skewers and broiled. Kebabs are also delicious when cooked over a charcoal grill.

1½ lb. ground lamb or beef

3 cloves garlic, chopped

1 tsp. fresh ginger, grated

1 green chili, finely chopped

1 medium onion, finely chopped

3 tbsp. chopped fresh coriander leaves

1 tbsp. plain yogurt (optional)

½ tsp. ground turmeric

1 tbsp. lemon juice

1 tsp. salt

1 tbsp. butter or margarine, melted

1. In a large bowl, combine all ingredients except melted butter. Use your hands to mix ingredients well until mixture is fairly stiff. Cover bowl and let stand at room temperature for 30 minutes.

2. Preheat broiler. Lightly grease 12 skewers with the melted butter. Wet hands slightly and shape small pieces of meat mixture into oblong shapes around skewers, about two on each skewer.

3. Line the bottom of a broiler pan with aluminum foil. Place skewers across broiler pan.

4. Place broiler pan in oven about 6 inches from heat. Broil kebabs for about 5 minutes, or until well browned. Turn skewers and broil kebabs for an additional 4 minutes.

5. Place skewers on a platter and serve.

Preparation time: 55 minutes
Cooking time: 10 minutes
Serves 4 to 6

Yogurt Chicken / Murg Dahi

Yogurt gives this dish from northern India a wonderful flavor and also makes the meat very tender. The yogurt and spice flavors will penetrate the chicken if you skin it as Indian cooks always do. To remove the skin, hold a chicken piece in one hand and pull hard on the loose skin with the other hand. A paper towel will help you to get a good grip.*

3½ to 4 lbs. chicken pieces, skinned

1 tsp. salt

1 green chili, finely chopped

1 c. (8 oz.) plain yogurt

¼ c. fresh coriander leaves, chopped

1 tbsp. fresh ginger, chopped

3 or 4 cloves garlic, chopped

¼ c. (½ stick) butter or margarine, melted

1. Prick chicken pieces all over with a fork and place in a large bowl. In a small bowl, combine salt, chili, yogurt, coriander leaves, ginger, and garlic and mix well. Pour over chicken, cover bowl, and refrigerate for six hours or overnight.

2. To cook chicken, preheat oven to 400°F. Pour half the melted butter into a roasting pan. Put chicken into pan and pour yogurt mixture on top. Place pan in middle of oven and roast for about 20 minutes. Reduce heat to 350°F and continue roasting, basting frequently with remaining butter and pan juices, for about 30 minutes, or until chicken is done.

3. Remove chicken and place on a serving platter. Pour sauce over chicken and serve immediately.

*After handling raw chicken or other poultry, always remember to thoroughly wash your hands, utensils, and preparation area with soapy, hot water. Also, when checking chicken for doneness, slice a piece down the middle to make sure the meat is white (not pink) all the way through.

Preparation time: 10 minutes
Refrigeration time: 6 hours
Cooking time: 50 to 60 minutes
Serves 4 to 6

Spicy Fried Fish/Muchli Masala

India's coastal waters produce many fish, such as pomfret, that are not found in other parts of the world. For this tasty fish recipe, you can use sole, haddock, or any other white fish. Spicy fried fish is a dish from southern India, and it uses what is called a "wet" masala—spices mixed with water or other liquids to form a paste. Southern Indian cooks often prepare their spices in this way instead of using a mixture of dry spices.

2 lbs. white-fish fillets, fresh or frozen

2 cloves garlic, chopped

1 tsp. salt

1 tsp. grated fresh ginger

½ tsp. ground turmeric

½ tsp. black pepper

¼ tsp. cayenne pepper

2 tsp. lemon juice

¼ c. vegetable oil (for frying)

fresh coriander or parsley, for garnish

lemon wedges, for garnish

1. Rinse fish under cool running water and pat dry with paper towels.

2. In a small bowl, combine garlic, salt, ginger, turmeric, and black and cayenne peppers with lemon juice. Stir to form a paste.

3. Rub paste on both sides of fish fillets and let stand uncovered at room temperature for 20 minutes.

4. In a heavy skillet, heat oil over medium-high heat. Carefully add fish to skillet. Fry fish about 5 minutes, or until bottom side is golden brown. With a spatula, turn fish and fry other side about 5 minutes, or until golden brown.*

5. Place fish on a platter and garnish with fresh coriander or parsley and lemon wedges.

*For a healthier version of this recipe, omit Step 4. Instead, brush each fillet with a little canola oil. Place fish on a cookie sheet or in a casserole dish and broil in the oven for 5 minutes on each side, or until fish flakes when pulled with a fork and is no longer transparent.

Preparation time: 25 minutes
Cooking time: 10 minutes
Serves 4

Vegetarian Dishes

Generally, people in India eat far less meat than do other people around the world. The emphasis on meatless dining has led to a unique cuisine of vegetarian delights. Indian vegetarian recipes are known to surprise and satisfy even those unaccustomed to meatless meals.

Working with a few key ingredients, Indian cooks have created amazingly varied and flavorful dishes from simple staples. One of the most important staples of the Indian diet is *dal*, the Hindi word for "pulses," those versatile beans, lentils, and peas.

Many Indian dals are not available in the United States, but the ones used in these recipes can be obtained at supermarkets, Indian or Middle Eastern markets, cooperative groceries, or health food stores. Most Indians have some kind of dal at almost every meal. As a protein source, eaten with a starchy food like bread or rice and a milk product like yogurt, dal is a key part of a healthy, well-balanced diet.

Cayenne pepper, cumin, and turmeric spice up a sauce base of coconut milk and lentils to create this pumpkin curry. (Recipe on page 46.)

Pumpkin Curry / *Sambar*

The Indian curry served in most Western countries is usually a rice dish covered with a thick, yellow sauce containing commercial curry powder. In authentic Indian cooking, there is no specific dish called curry, but there are many dishes with sauces, each made with its own special spices and ingredients. The delicious sauce in pumpkin curry is made with coconut milk and lentils. If you can't get fresh pumpkin, try making this southern Indian specialty with a winter squash such as acorn or hubbard.

I small pumpkin or winter squash
  (about 3 c. chopped)

I c. lentils, brown or split red

4 c. water

I tsp. cayenne pepper

½ tsp. ground cumin

¼ tsp. ground turmeric

½ tsp. salt

½ c. coconut milk*

I tbsp. vegetable oil

¼ tsp. ground fenugreek

¼ tsp. black mustard seeds

I large onion, thinly sliced

I curry leaf (optional)

1. For pumpkin, cut into quarters, scrape out seeds, cut off peel, and chop into 1-inch squares. For squash, first bake whole for 20 minutes on the middle rack of a 400°F oven. Cool, then quarter, scrape out seeds, cut off peel, and chop.

2. Place lentils in a colander and rinse thoroughly with cold water. Remove any inedible objects from lentils while washing.**

3. Put 4 cups of water in a large kettle. Add cayenne pepper, cumin, turmeric, and salt and bring to a boil. Add lentils, cover, and lower heat. Simmer for about 30 minutes, or until lentils are tender. (If you are using split red lentils, they will cook in about 15 to 20 minutes.)

4. Add pumpkin squares to lentils. Cover and simmer 15 to 20 minutes, or until pumpkin is tender.

5. Add coconut milk to kettle and stir. As soon as mixture begins to boil, remove from heat and set aside.

6. In a skillet, heat oil over medium-high heat. Add fenugreek, mustard seeds, onion slices, and curry leaf and fry for 4 to 5 minutes, or until mixture is brown.

7. Add onion-and-spice mixture to kettle. Cover kettle and let stand 5 minutes.

8. Stir pumpkin curry before serving over rice.

**In cooking with lentils or chickpeas, be sure to examine the pulses to remove small stones, twigs, and other inedible objects before cooking.*

Preparation time: 25 to 30 minutes
Cooking time: 60 minutes
Serves 6 to 8

*If you can't find canned coconut milk, combine ½ c. flaked coconut and ½ c. boiling water in a bowl. Cover and let soak for 5 minutes. (Alternatively, if an electric blender is available, blend coconut and boiling water for 1 minute.) Place mixture in a sieve over the back of a spoon to get all the liquid out. Set coconut milk aside and discard flaked coconut.

Curried Chickpeas / *Channa Dal*

1½ c. chickpeas, washed and drained*

5 c. water

1 tsp. ground turmeric

½ tsp. ground cumin

1 tsp. ground coriander

½ tsp. cayenne pepper (optional)

3 tbsp. butter or margarine

1 tsp. cumin seeds

1 medium onion, chopped

1 clove garlic, chopped

1 tbsp. grated fresh ginger

1 tsp. garam masala (optional)

2 tbsp. chopped fresh coriander leaves

*For speedier preparation, purchase canned, rather than dried, chickpeas at the supermarket. Using two 14-oz. cans of presoaked chickpeas eliminates the first step and reduces the cooking time in the second and fourth steps by half.

1. Put chickpeas in a bowl, examine for inedible objects. Add enough cold water to cover and soak overnight.

2. To cook, drain chickpeas. Place chickpeas, 5 c. water, turmeric, cumin, coriander, and cayenne in a heavy saucepan and bring to a boil over medium-high heat. Reduce heat to low, cover pan, and simmer for about 1 hour.

3. In a large saucepan, melt butter over medium heat. Add cumin seeds and cook for 1 minute. Add the onion, garlic, and ginger and cook for about 5 minutes, stirring frequently, or until onion turns golden brown.

4. Add chickpeas and cooking liquid to onion mixture. Turn heat to high and bring to a boil, stirring constantly. Cover pan, reduce heat to low, and simmer 30 minutes, or until chickpeas are tender but not mushy.

5. Add garam masala and mix well.

6. Place chickpeas in a serving dish and sprinkle with chopped coriander leaves.

Soaking time: overnight
Preparation time: 10 minutes
Cooking time: 90 minutes
Serves 6 to 8

Lentils with Garlic and Onion / Masoor Dal

3 c. water

I c. split red or brown lentils, washed and drained *

½ tsp. ground turmeric

⅛ tsp. cayenne pepper (optional)

3 tbsp. vegetable or peanut oil

½ tsp. whole cumin seeds

3 cloves garlic, finely chopped

I medium onion, chopped

I tsp. salt

1. Combine water, lentils, turmeric, and cayenne in a large saucepan or kettle and bring to a boil over medium-high heat. Cover pan, turn heat to low, and simmer for about 30 minutes, or until lentils are tender. (If you are using split red lentils, they will cook in about 15 to 20 minutes.)

2. Meanwhile, in another saucepan, heat oil over medium heat. Add cumin seeds and stir. Add garlic, onion, and salt and continue stirring for about 5 minutes, or until onion begins to brown.

3. When lentils are cooked, add onion mixture to them. Mix well and simmer for 5 additional minutes before serving.

Preparation time: 10 minutes
Cooking time: 35 minutes
Serves 6 to 8

*Split red lentils are known in Hindi as masoor dal. They may be found in Indian or Middle Eastern markets as well as in some larger supermarkets. This dish tastes wonderful made with almost any variety of lentil.

Carrots with Grated Coconut/ *Gajar Nariyal*

The kitchen equipment of a southern Indian cook often includes a special utensil used to scrape coconut meat from the inside of the hard shell. Since coconuts may not be readily available, the recipes in this book call for prepared coconut products. Unsweetened flaked coconut can usually be obtained in a cooperative grocery or a health food store. The flaked coconut carried in most supermarkets is flavored with sugar, but it can be used if the unsweetened variety is not available.

6 carrots, peeled and cut into thin round slices

½ c. flaked coconut

1 tsp. ground cumin

2 tsp. ground coriander

2 tsp. ground turmeric

3 tbsp. vegetable oil

1 tsp. black mustard seeds*

¾ c. water

¼ c. ground peanuts (optional)

1. In a bowl, combine carrots, coconut, cumin, coriander, and turmeric and mix well.

2. In a skillet with a lid, heat oil over medium-high heat. Add mustard seeds and fry for about 3 minutes, or until seeds pop. (Hold or place lid loosely over skillet so seeds don't pop out of the pan.)

3. Add carrot-coconut mixture and fry for 10 minutes. Add water, lower heat, and simmer for about 10 minutes, or until carrots are tender.

4. Mix ground peanuts into carrots, if desired, and serve steaming hot.

Preparation time: 15 minutes
Cooking time: 25 minutes
Serves 4 to 6

* This simple vegetable dish uses black mustard seeds, which have a more delicate flavor than the ordinary yellow seeds. Yellow mustard seeds can be used if you can't get black ones, but you might want to use only ½ tsp. instead.

Accompaniments

Indian cuisine seeks a satisfying balance of tastes—sweet, sour, salty, and three types of bitter. This goal comes from Ayurveda, a 5,000-year-old science that focuses on food and natural remedies as tools to achieve a long and healthy life. According to Ayurvedic belief, eating layered and balanced flavors encourages proper digestion and the release of positive, nurturing energy from the foods we eat.

Accompaniments like raita, chutney, bread, and rice are crucial to achieving this coveted balance, so they are a prominent part of every Indian meal. Raita is a cool, crunchy topping of yogurt mixed with vegetables or fruit. Indian cooks usually make their own yogurt out of water buffalo milk. Chutneys are sweet, sour, mild or fiery delicacies served with every Indian meal to contrast with the main dish. Bread and balls of rice are practical accompaniments that diners use to scoop up the juicy sauces, as well as to neutralize some of the sharper flavors.

Chapatis—a flat unleavened whole wheat bread—are edible utensils, standard at every northern Indian meal. (Recipe on pages 54–55.)

Unleavened Whole Wheat Bread/ *Puris*

The breads that Indians eat are very different from the plump, crusty loaves that are familiar to Westerners. Most Indian bread has no leavening agent like yeast, so it does not rise when it is cooked. Puris and chapatis, the most popular kinds of Indian bread, are flat pancakes that resemble thick Mexican tortillas. Like tortillas, they are cooked on a very hot griddle and are best eaten right after they are made.

2½ c. whole wheat flour

2 tbsp. butter or margarine

1 tsp. salt

1 c. lukewarm water

2 tbsp. vegetable oil

1. Put 2 c. flour into a large mixing bowl.

2. Cut butter into small pieces. Make a hollow in the center of the flour and add butter. Rub butter into flour with your fingertips until mixture looks like large bread crumbs.

3. Mix salt into water. Add enough water, a little at a time, to flour mixture to make a firm (but not stiff) dough.

4. Knead dough in bowl for about 5 or 10 minutes. Cover bowl with a damp cloth and let stand at room temperature for at least 1 hour.

5. Divide dough into pieces about the size of walnuts. Roll each piece into a smooth ball with your hands.

6. Sprinkle remaining ½ c. flour onto a flat surface. With a floured rolling pin, roll out each ball until it resembles a thin pancake, about ⅛-inch thick.

7. In a large skillet, heat vegetable oil over medium-high heat.* Carefully place each puri in oil, one at a time. Using a spatula, carefully splash oil onto puris while frying. This will make puris puff up and will cook the top side of each one. Fry puris about 2 minutes, or until golden brown on both sides. Remove puris from skillet and drain on paper towels.

8. Continue cooking puris, one at a time. Wrap the cooked ones in a towel to keep them warm.

9. Brush cooked puris with butter and serve warm.

Preparation time: 35 minutes (plus 1 hour standing time)
Cooking time: 30 minutes
Makes 12 to 15 puris

* To make chapatis, cook each circle of dough in a skillet without oil. When small brown spots appear on the bottom of the dough and the edges begin to curl up (about 1 minute), turn the chapati over with a spatula. Cook another 1 to 2 minutes. Serve hot.

Spiced Rice/ *Pulao*

This rice dish from northern India is similar to the pilafs popular in Middle Eastern countries. It is a tasty combination of rice with spices, raisins, and nuts. The best kind of Indian rice to use is basmati, a long-grained rice with a delicate, nutty flavor.

2 tbsp. vegetable or peanut oil

½ medium onion, thinly sliced

5 whole cloves

½ stick cinnamon

5 cardamom pods

½ tsp. ground coriander

1 c. basmati or other long-grain rice, rinsed and well-drained

½ tsp. salt

2 c. boiling water

1 tbsp. butter or margarine

¼ c. raisins

2 tbsp. blanched slivered almonds or cashews

1. In a large frying pan, heat oil over medium-high heat. Add onion and cook about 5 minutes, or until soft.

2. Add spices. Reduce heat to medium-low and cook for 1 minute. Stir in rice and fry until coated with oil.

3. Add salt and 2 c. boiling water and bring mixture to a boil over medium heat.

4. When rice begins to boil, cover pan, reduce heat to low, and cook about 20–25 minutes, or until all water is absorbed and rice is tender.

5. When rice is cooked, heat butter in a small skillet over medium-high heat. Add raisins and nuts and fry for 1 or 2 minutes, or until raisins are plump and nuts are golden brown.

6. Stir raisin-nut mixture into rice and serve immediately. (Don't forget that there are whole spices in this dish that you will want to remove before eating.)

Preparation time: 10 minutes
Cooking time: 30 minutes
Serves 6 to 8

Banana Yogurt / Kela ka Raita

1½ c. (12 oz.) plain yogurt

2 large bananas, peeled and sliced

¼ c. flaked coconut

1 green chili, finely chopped

1 tsp. lemon juice

½ tsp. garam masala or ¼ tsp. each
ground coriander and ground
cinnamon

¼ tsp. salt

1 tsp. finely chopped fresh coriander
leaves

1. In a medium mixing bowl,
beat yogurt until smooth. Stir
in bananas, coconut, chili,
lemon juice, garam masala,
and salt. Cover bowl and chill
at least 1 hour.

2. Just before serving, sprinkle
coriander leaves over raita.*

Preparation time: 15 minutes
Refrigeration time: 60 minutes
Serves 4

*For an energizing breakfast raita, combine a selection
of seasonal fruits with banana yogurt and garnish with
a handful of slivered almonds or granola.*

Cucumber and Mint Yogurt/ *Kheera ka Raita**

3 c. (24 oz.) plain yogurt

I peeled cucumber, chopped

3 tbsp. fresh mint leaves, finely chopped

½ tsp. ground cumin

I tsp. salt

¼ tsp. black pepper

⅛ tsp. cayenne pepper (optional)

1. In a mixing bowl, beat yogurt until smooth. Stir in remaining ingredients.

2. Cover and chill at least 1 hour before serving.

Preparation time: 10 minutes
Refrigeration time: 60 minutes
Serves 6

Cucumber and Tomato Yogurt/ *Kheera–Tamatar Raita*

2 c. (16 oz.) plain yogurt

I medium tomato, chopped

I peeled cucumber, chopped

I small onion, chopped

3 tbsp. chopped fresh coriander

salt and pepper to taste

dash of cayenne pepper (optional)

1. In a bowl, beat yogurt until smooth. Combine yogurt with remaining ingredients and mix well.

2. Cover bowl and chill at least 1 hour before serving.

Preparation time: 15 minutes
Refrigeration time: 60 minutes
Serves 4

* *The raita recipes on this page also make healthy, delicious dressings. Sprinkle some cucumber and tomato yogurt over a fresh, mixed green salad or use cucumber and mint yogurt in place of mayonnaise on a deli-style sandwich.*

Fresh Coriander Chutney/Dhanya Chatni

Fresh coriander chutney has the tangy, slightly sour taste of the green coriander leaves. This popular chutney is made fresh daily in many Indian households.

3 c. fresh coriander leaves, coarsely chopped

½ green chili, chopped

2 tbsp. lemon juice

¼ tsp. salt

½ tsp. ground cumin

¼ tsp. black pepper

1. Combine all ingredients in a blender and blend until smooth.

2. Put chutney in a small glass or nonmetallic bowl to serve.

Preparation time: 15 minutes
Makes ½ c.

Apple Chutney / Shebki Chatni

Apple chutney is a sweet, cooked chutney that will keep for several weeks in the refrigerator.

3 tart cooking apples, peeled, cored, and coarsely chopped*

1 c. chopped dried fruits, such as peaches, apricots, or pears, or a combination of fruits

½ c. golden raisins

3 cloves garlic, chopped

2 tsp. finely chopped fresh ginger

1 tsp. salt

¼ tsp. cayenne pepper

1 c. white-wine vinegar

1½ c. sugar

1. In a heavy saucepan, combine all ingredients and mix well. Bring to a boil over medium-high heat.

2. Reduce heat and simmer, stirring occasionally, for about 45 minutes, or until mixture is thick.

3. Remove saucepan from heat and cool chutney to room temperature.

4. Pour chutney into a nonmetallic, covered container and refrigerate until ready to use.

Preparation time: 10 minutes
Cooking time: 50 minutes
Makes 3 c.

Apples come in many varieties, each with distinct characteristics. For chutney, although almost any apple will work, tart cooking apples turn out best. (Avoid Red Delicious for this recipe. They don't cook well.) Choose firm, unbruised fruit of the Granny Smith, Golden Delicious, McIntosh, or Fuji variety.

Holiday and Festival Food

Most Indian families do not eat desserts on a regular basis. On holidays and other special occasions, however, treats flow from the kitchen. Common dessert ingredients include milk, sugar, cardamom, and nuts. Holiday food is almost always vegetarian. That way no one is excluded from the feast as families and friends gather together to partake in good company and good food.

The following recipes introduce the typical fare of particular holidays and festivals. Many of the dishes reappear at several special occasions throughout the year. You don't have to wait for a festival to enjoy these goodies. To imitate an Indian celebration, whip up a dish or two, look your best, and invite friends and family to join you.

Indian toffee, called barfi, is a favorite treat for Diwali, the festival of lights usually celebrated in October. (Recipe on page 64.)

Indian Toffee / *Barfi*

Families exchange plates of sweets during Diwali. Barfi, a favorite treat at many celebrations, is quick and easy to make, which allows more time for socializing.

½ c. sugar

½ c. water

3 oz. condensed milk

I c. mixed nuts, chopped*

¾ c. bread crumbs

I tbsp. butter

½ tsp. vanilla

1. Bring sugar and water to a boil. Remove from heat.

2. Add remaining ingredients and stir until mixture thickens and resembles dough.

3. While mixture is hot, roll it out in a layer ½- to ¾-inch thick on a greased surface or a piece of wax paper. Immediately cut into squares. Serve warm or at room temperature.

Preparation time: 15 to 20 minutes
Serves 6

You can use a variety of nuts in this toffee, depending on the items on hand and those you would like to purchase at the store. Try any combination of almonds, cashews, peanuts, walnuts, pistachios, and sesame seeds.

Sweetened Rice / *Pongal*

Southern Indian cooks serve this dish to commemorate the rice harvest festival. Pongal can be sweet or salty, but this sweet version is more common. Although Indians wait for the mixture to boil over, pongal tastes just as good when it stays in the pot.

I c. basmati rice, or other long-grain white rice

2 c. milk

¼ c. water

1½ c. jaggery, or loosely packed brown sugar

3 tbsp. ghee or butter

¼ c. coconut, grated or flaked

3 tbsp. raisins

2 tbsp. cashews or almonds, sliced

I tsp. ground cardamom

⅛ tsp. ground nutmeg

1. Rinse the rice, soak it in water for 15 minutes, and drain.

2. Bring milk and water to a boil.

3. Add rice, cook over a medium heat, stirring frequently, until rice is tender. (If the liquid is absorbed before the mixture softens, add water in ¼ c. quantities until rice is fully cooked.)

4. Reduce heat and stir in jaggery or brown sugar until thoroughly combined. Add 2 tbsp. of the ghee or butter.

5. In a separate small pan, fry the coconut, raisins, and nuts in the remaining ghee or butter until mixture turns golden. Transfer to the rice mixture.

6. Sprinkle in the cardamom and nutmeg. Stir well and serve hot.

Preparation time: 20 minutes
Cooking time: 50 minutes
Serves 4 to 6

Stuffed Sweet Bread/ *Puran Poli*

Many Indians reenergize during Holi with this crepelike treat, which also is featured several weeks later at Ugadi, a festival celebrating the new year.

Stuffing:

2 c. yellow split peas, soaked in
  water for 4 hours, then drained

¼ c. water

2 c. jaggery, or to taste

1 tsp. ground cardamom

½ tsp. ground nutmeg

Dough:

2 c. flour

3 tbsp. oil

½ tsp. turmeric

½–1 c. water

butter to serve**

*If the liquid is absorbed before the mixture softens, add water in ¼ c. quantities until peas are fully cooked.

**These treats are delicious when topped with a dollop of butter and served warm with a glass of cold milk.

1. To prepare the stuffing, cook split peas in ¼ c. water until soft.* Drain well. Add jaggery and mix well. Mash into a fine paste.

2. Heat mixture on low until it thickens into a lump, stirring continuously.

3. Remove from heat. Stir in ground spices. Roll mixture into 20 equal-sized stuffing balls. Set aside.

4. Mix flour, oil, and turmeric. Knead water into the mixture, ¼ c. at a time, until a soft, sticky dough forms. Divide into 20 equal balls.

5. Use a floured rolling pin or your palm to flatten each ball into a circle.

6. Place a stuffing ball in the center of each circle and wrap the dough around it to create a poli. Repeat.

7. Flour a workspace and roll out each poli into a 6-inch circle.

8. Roast both sides of each poli on a hot griddle until brown and fragrant. No oil is necessary.

Soaking time: 4 hours
Preparation and cooking time: 60 minutes
Serves 6 to 8

Nutty Milk Shake / *Thandai*

This beverage helps Indians cool down after participating in the festivities during Holi and Diwali.

¼ tsp. anise seeds*

2–3 peppercorns

½ tsp. ground cardamom

1 stick cinnamon

¼ c. cashews

¼ c. almonds

¼ c. pistachios

1 tbsp. poppy seeds

1 qt. milk

½ c. sugar or honey (plus extra to taste)

*Anise is the strong-tasting spice used to flavor black licorice. It's available in the spice section of most supermarkets.

1. Use an electric food processor to grind anise seeds, peppercorns, cardamom, and cinnamon.

2. Add the nuts and poppy seeds. Process until the ingredients form a smooth paste. You may need to transfer the mixture to a bowl and use the back of a large wooden spoon to break down any remaining lumps.

3. In a saucepan, heat milk and sugar over low heat until sugar dissolves.

4. Add the ground spice-nuts mixture to the milk and stir well. Heat for 3 to 4 minutes.

5. Remove from heat and let liquid cool at room temperature, allowing it to steep and soften the nuts.

6. Refrigerate until chilled, at least one hour. Before serving, check liquid for sweetness and adjust as necessary with more honey or sugar. Stir well or whip in a blender and serve cold.

Preparation time: 15 minutes
Refrigeration time: 1 hour
Serves 4 to 6

Vermicelli Pudding/Sevian Ki Kheer

Indian Muslims eat this sweet treat after moonrise to celebrate the breaking of the Ramadan fast. The pudding is created from vermicelli—long, very thin spaghetti.

4 oz. vermicelli

1 tbsp. ghee or unsalted butter

¼ c. raisins

¼ c. sliced almonds

2½ c. whole milk

½ c. sugar

½ tsp. ground cardamom

1. Break vermicelli into 3-inch pieces.

2. Heat ghee in heavy saucepan. Add raisins, almonds, and vermicelli pieces. Brown lightly.

3. Add milk and bring to a boil, stirring frequently.

4. Reduce heat and simmer vermicelli until soft (about 10 minutes).

5. Stir in sugar and cardamom, remove from heat, and allow to thicken.

6. Serve warm.

Preparation time: 5 minutes
Cooking time: 15 minutes
Serves 4

Index

About the Author

Vijay Madavan was born and raised in Malaysia. Her grandparents settled there after growing up in Kerala, India. Madavan remembers well the Indian influences of both her parents and grandparents, especially in the field of cooking. As a girl, Madavan (along with her two sisters) learned the art of Indian cooking from her mother and still practices it today.

After receiving her B.A. in Business Administration from Stamford College in London, Madavan moved to Minnesota in 1981. Madavan has remarried since the death of her first husband, Steve. She lives in Hopkins, Minnesota, with her second husband, Thomas.

Photo Acknowledgments
The photographs in this book are reproduced courtesy of: © Earl & Nazima Kowall/CORBIS, pp. 2–3, 24; © Walter and Louiseann Pietrowicz/September 8th Stock, pp. 4 (left), 5 (both), 6, 16, 37, 38, 43, 44, 49, 52, 57, 62, 67; © Robert L. and Diane Wolfe, pp. 4 (right), 28, 34; FAO photo/P. Gigli, p. 11; © Bob Krist/CORBIS, p. 12; © AFP/CORBIS, p. 15.

Cover photos: © Robert L. and Diane Wolfe, front top, bottom left, spine; © Walter and Louiseann Pietrowicz/September 8th Stock, back.

The illustrations on pages 7, 17, 25, 29, 31, 35, 36, 39, 41, 42, 45, 47, 48, 50, 51, 53, 55, 58, 59, 61, 63, 64, 66 and 68 and the map on page 8 are by Tim Seeley.

DATE		